NHS
market
futures

D1477567

NHS MARKET FUTURES

Expl

Ri

This paper outlines some of the major challenges that face policy-makers in the NHS as they implement their reform agenda, as well as options for meeting these challenges. The paper also considers how the introduction of market systems into the NHS may help or hinder the achievement of the core aims of the NHS.

Published by:

King's Fund
11–13 Cavendish Square
London W1G 0AN
www.kingsfund.org.uk

First published 2005

ISBN 1 85717 534 4

A catalogue record for this publication is available from the British Library.

Available from:

King's Fund Publications
11–13 Cavendish Square
London W1G 0AN
Tel: 020 7307 2591
Fax: 020 7307 2801
Email: publications@kingsfund.org.uk
www.kingsfund.org.uk/publications

Edited by Eleanor Stanley
Typeset by Lucy Latchmore
Printed and bound in Great Britain

Contents

Foreword

The National Health Service in England has embarked on one of the most radical and far reaching set of reforms in its history. The success or failure of this endeavour will determine the future of the NHS and perhaps even whether it has one.

In some ways, the government's intentions and programmes are clear. It wants to make health care more accessible, more efficient and more responsive. The aim is to create a service that meets the rising expectations of patients and public, and yet remains affordable within the constraints of a tax-funded system.

The means by which to achieve this have also been well rehearsed – even if they remain little understood among the wider public and even health service staff. While unprecedented extra funding, additional central targets and a national framework of regulation have brought about significant improvements during the last five years, there is now a belief that further, more fundamental change is needed, including more powerful incentives to drive up performance.

Hence the introduction of market-style mechanisms, the plan to move away from monopolies delivering local services to a diverse range of providers, and the avowed aim of devolving power and decision-making to a local level.

The difficulty is that these initiatives raise as many questions as they answer. In addition, they form only part of the change agenda, which also includes a a radical change to the pay system, the biggest IT reform programme ever seen and, more recently, a major structural reorganisation.

This short report by Richard Lewis and Jennifer Dixon is designed to stimulate debate around the market reforms by setting out some of the challenges to be addressed and identifying some of the uncertainties, tensions and contradictions that are inevitable when bringing about change in such a complex enterprise.

Over the next few months, the King's Fund will be publishing further reports and holding a number of events to explore these issues in greater depth and look for some practical solutions.

If you would like to be kept up-to-date with this programme of work or find out more about any other aspect of the King's Fund's work please sign up for email updates at www.kingsfund.org.uk/updates.

Niall Dickson
Chief Executive

About the authors

Richard Lewis is Fellow in Health Policy at the King's Fund. He carries out policy analysis and research, with a special interest in foundation trusts, commissioning, US managed care, patient safety and primary care. He is also an independent health care consultant. He has a background in health service management, and spent several years as executive director of a large health authority in south-west London. Richard has a PhD in health policy.

Jennifer Dixon is Director of Policy at the King's Fund. She has researched and written widely on health care reform, in the United Kingdom and internationally. Her background is in clinical medicine and policy analysis, and she has a PhD in health services research. She was Harkness Fellow in New York in 1990, and Policy Advisor to the Chief Executive of the National Health Service between 1998 and 2000. Jennifer is currently a board member of both the Audit Commission and the Healthcare Commission.

Introduction

There seems little doubt that since 1997, the NHS in England has improved significantly across a range of important domains (King's Fund 2005, Healthcare Commission 2005). For this, the government and the NHS deserve congratulation. However, Prime Minister Tony Blair's initial aim to 'transform' the quality of service received by patients in the NHS remains elusive. While some areas have improved, significant problems remain.

The traditional response to concern about the quality of care in the NHS has been that the NHS is underfunded. Partly to neuter this claim, and partly as a response to the Wanless Inquiry (Wanless 2002), the government agreed to unprecedented increases in funding from 1999. The NHS budget in England has grown significantly, from £37 billion in 1998/99 (Department of Health 1998) to £76 billion in 2004/05 (Department of Health 2005a). But the government accompanied this investment with a requirement to reform, with the NHS Plan forming the first blueprint of the reform agenda (Department of Health 2000).

Since then, there has been a raft of further policy developments. Arguably, the most significant of these relate to the attempt to devolve power from the centre to the local NHS, and to introduce market-style incentives to providers, to prompt improvement. As a result, the NHS is in transition. Recent reforms are transforming the NHS from a public monopoly insurer and provider of health care, governed largely from Whitehall, to an insurer with devolved commissioners buying services from a mixed market of providers (*see* box, pp 2–3).

POLICIES REDUCING THE DEPARTMENT OF HEALTH'S CONTROL OVER THE NHS IN ENGLAND

Creating local purchasing power

- **Devolving resources from the Department of Health to local primary care trusts (PCTs)** 85 per cent of NHS resources are now spent by PCTs.

- **Encouraging further devolution of spending decisions to GP practices** The government target is for all practices to be commissioning almost all care for their patients by the end of 2006.

- **Reducing capacity at the centre and regionally** The government target is to achieve a 40 per cent reduction in the number of Department of Health staff as well as a reduction in the number of strategic health authorities by 2007.

- **Introducing payment by results** This is a new system by which hospitals are paid for operations or treatments only when they have done them, with the price fixed by a national tariff for specific procedures. The system is designed to encourage providers to keep costs low and make their care and facilities more attractive to patients. The system is being rolled out slowly – covering only a very small number of procedures for most hospitals in 2003, increasing to 90 per cent of hospital care by 2008.

- **Extending patient choice** To date, choice of provider has been limited to patients who have been waiting long times for certain procedures. But from December 2005, all patients needing planned surgery or treatment will be able to choose from five providers, and from 2008 the government has promised that patients will be able to choose any provider meeting NHS standards and prices.

continued opposite

Encouraging a mixed economy of 'autonomous' providers

■ **The creation of NHS foundation trusts as part of the 2003 Health and Social Care Act** This legislation freed a number of NHS hospitals from direct control of the Department of Health and enabled them to borrow capital, sell assets and retain in-year surpluses. Governed by a board that includes representatives of their local community, foundation trusts are intended to be more responsive to local needs and have more autonomy to ensure those needs are met. So far, 32 NHS hospitals have become foundation trusts.

■ **Increasing the role of private-sector providers** While still currently providing only a small proportion of care for NHS patients, the government is expanding the role of the independent sector through nationally awarded contracts (for example, for new diagnostic and treatment centres) and by enabling patients to choose any provider for planned surgery that meets NHS standards and prices.

■ **Introducing competition within primary and community care services** Department of Health guidance issued in July 2005 proposed that by the end of 2008, PCTs should no longer directly provide their own services. More details are anticipated in the forthcoming white paper on 'out-of-hospital' care.

■ **Establishing independent regulation of providers** the Healthcare Commission was created in 2004 as an independent organisation inspecting all health care providers and providing information to the public about the quality of that care. The Commission for Social Care Inspection provides a similar function for social care services. And Monitor is the independent regulator of foundation trusts, authorising their establishment and, partly through Healthcare Commission inspections, monitoring their activities.

This paper outlines some of the major challenges that face policy-makers in the NHS in the short to medium term, as they seek to implement the reform agenda and consider their options for meeting them. However, the successful implementation of the government's health policies does not guarantee the achievement of the core aim of the NHS: the equitable and efficient provision of high-quality care to patients, regardless of ability to pay. The policy course on which the government has embarked may maximise some aims at the expense of others. We also consider some of the trade-offs that may be required as current policies evolve.

Complexity of the reform agenda

The reforms are complex, and the scale of change is vast. Many reforms are not yet implemented. However, it is clear that the results of their interaction may be at best unpredictable and at worst perverse. There is a huge job to be done to monitor the effects of change, spot problems, and manage risk appropriately. To fail to do so risks reforms being stalled – or even reversed – before their value is known, if the service (or some politicians) lose their nerve in the face of early and very public failures.

These issues are pressing. The financial environment is already challenging. Cost pressures arising from pay modernisation and the reduction in waiting times for care have been expensive, and have absorbed the majority of the additional resources made available to the NHS (King's Fund 2005). New accounting rules mean that NHS organisations have to be much more transparent in reporting their end-of-year financial position. The implementation of payment by results has challenged many a finance and information department in ensuring that activity is recorded and costed accurately, and paid for by commissioners.

The National Audit Office/Audit Commission report into the NHS accounts 2003/04 showed the significant extent of the problem throughout England (National Audit Office/Audit Commission 2005), backed up by increasing reports of financial failure (Bamford 2005, McFarland 2005). The 2005 'star ratings' allocated by the Healthcare Commission show, for the first time, a drop in the number of hospital trusts achieving three stars and third of hospitals in deficit to a cumulative total of £500 million (Healthcare Commission 2005).

As they stand, the reforms have yet to be tested in practice. As we look further into the future, the unknowns become greater. For example, we simply cannot say how NHS hospitals and practice-based commissioners will respond to the new incentives that are before them. Already, concerns have emerged that these incentives will result in unexpected increases in activity. Therefore, further reform is likely to be needed to create a high-quality and cost-effective service for patients. This has to be done incrementally, but at the same time it is important to have a clearer overall picture of how the main elements and incentives in a health care system fit together. This picture is as yet only partially developed.

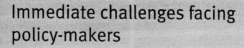

Immediate challenges facing policy-makers

Challenge 1: Implementing reforms and managing risks

From the government's perspective, the first major challenge is to oversee a successful implementation of the current reforms and to manage effectively the risks arising from their local implementation. In particular, this means dealing effectively with the significant financial instability facing NHS trusts and primary care trusts (PCTs) arising from the implementation of payment by results, patient choice and the entry into the NHS 'market' of private providers. The government desires a degree of financial instability – in theory, to promote greater efficiency and responsiveness among providers – but the loss of individual services, which may no longer appear viable, and the wholesale collapse of valuable institutions would not be advantageous.

To all this must be added an ambitious and rapid programme of organisational change announced in July 2005. This will create new roles for PCTs and strategic health authorities, which may be sensible in themselves, but which risk overloading the system at a time of unprecedented change, and diverting managerial attention away from operational issues.

Current policies will have complex interactions and unpredictable effects in different parts of the country, and will require significant and detailed monitoring, anticipation and interception of problems. How should this best be done, and to what extent, if at all, should the financial incentives be blunted in the face of significant instability? Furthermore, this 'market management' role is required at a time when the staffing contingent at the Department of Health has been cut by 40 per cent and strategic health authorities and PCTs are set to decline substantially in number.

Challenge 2: Avoiding inflating demand and hospitalisation

The second related challenge is that many of the current reforms, if left unchecked, risk inflating demand for NHS care. Under payment by results, providers of NHS care have a clear incentive to maximise activity and income. The international evidence of 'supplier-induced demand' is strong, and in England we have seen that new forms of care, such as the nurse-led health helpline NHS Direct, tend more to satisfy new patient demands rather than substitute for existing services (Munro *et al* 2000). In addition, the rights of patients to select their care provider are growing (to incorporate a choice of any recognised provider in the public or private sector by 2008) at the same time that waits for hospital treatment are reducing substantially. This also raises the prospect of a rapid increase in the demand for hospital services through a lowering of referral or admission thresholds.

While incentives to maximise productivity and reduce waiting times may be appropriate for elective care, they may be less effective – and may even be deleterious – for emergency care and services for patients with long-term conditions. Here, the avoidance of hospitalisation may be the key objective, yet commissioners, primary care providers and NHS trusts do not currently have strong incentives to work towards this aim. Much more detailed work needs to be done to design appropriate incentives for different parts of the health care system and ensure that perverse impacts are anticipated and minimised.

Challenge 3: Strengthening commissioning and primary care

The third related major challenge is how to strengthen commissioning and the provision of primary, community and social care that can enable patients to avoid unnecessary hospitalisation. A new White Paper on 'out-of-hospital care' (including social care) is promised. In addition, the recent document *Commissioning a Patient-Led NHS* (Department of Health 2005b) offers a direction of travel that involves introducing more market incentives to primary care and community services, and the spread of practice-based commissioning.

However, the paper leaves many important questions unanswered – for example, how can general practitioners really be fully engaged in managing resources? The government is now committed to introducing practice-based commissioning throughout the NHS in England, but has also indicated that practices will be involved at different levels. How can there be effective integration with social care when this is needed? To whom should commissioning bodies be accountable, and how could primary care staff be strongly encouraged to improve the quality of service offered? Similarly, the paper may not go far enough. Are there enough incentives in the system for commissioners to begin to make a significant impact on the design of care? Should competition be allowed between PCT commissioners, and should patients be allowed to choose between them?

Challenge 4: Developing regulation

The fourth major challenge is to clarify the type and extent of regulation and performance management that will be needed in the developing market of provision. The current regulatory environment is already crowded and may require streamlining, yet in some key regards our understanding of the ultimate goal of regulation is underdeveloped. In particular, how should the emerging 'market' best be regulated, and to what ends? What are the appropriate functions of a regulator, and how should these differ from the current regime of performance management? Should hospitals be allowed to merge horizontally with others or vertically with primary or community services, and what existing legislation has bearing on this? Who should set the NHS tariff of prices under payment by results, and how?

Underpinning these four challenges are two more fundamental, questions that need to be answered: where is the reform agenda heading, and what will the NHS look like in the medium term? Finding answers to these questions involves developing a clear vision for the NHS of the future, and understanding in particular how far competition and patient choice should be extended.

What might the future look like?

The overriding aims for the NHS of successive governments have remained remarkably stable, and a broad consensus has been sustained. In general, governments of all hues have characterised an ideal NHS as one that delivers equitable access to health care for patients according to their clinical needs, without regard for their ability to pay, and as efficiently as possible. In addition, the current government has committed itself to reducing the gap in health status between different social groups, while recognising that formal health services are only one factor in determining health status.

Where governments have departed from one another is in the means by which they believe these ends can best be achieved. In this, as we have outlined, the current government has now placed its faith in a variety of tools, including, most recently, an increased use of market-style incentives (going further, in this regard, than previous Conservative governments). However, as we have suggested, the government faces many complex questions about the consequences and future direction of the policies that it has initiated.

Policy-makers are faced with an array of different visions for the NHS of the future, each based on different assumptions as to what will best deliver 'modern' health services that meet the needs of increasingly informed patients. Policy-makers need to locate their preferred position on that spectrum.

At one extreme lies a wholly market-based health system where competition rules and light-touch regulation ensures the health of that market, together with basic consumer protection. Plurality of provision and commissioning with strong incentives to compete may be features of such a system. At the other end of the spectrum is located a nationally

planned, owned and provided service, governed from the centre.
The government has clearly signalled a determination to move away
from this. Yet how far towards a market model will health services
be encouraged to move?

There is no simple, predictable or inevitable answer to this question.
It will depend in part upon:
- the values and ideological preferences of the government
- how the reform project is led and managed
- the level of political support for the policy in Parliament
- the implementation and impact of the reforms already underway
- public perceptions of reform and the service offered
- evidence of the quality of care
- satisfaction of the public with health services in comparable
  Organisation for Economic Co-operation and Development (OECD)
  countries.

Many of these factors are beyond the control of the government of the
day, although they can be shaped by them. In the immediate term,
there are only a fixed number of levers that can be employed to improve
performance in the NHS, including national targets and performance
management; financial incentives for institutions, managers and
professionals; regulation; professional (non-financial) incentives;
and formal systems of public accountability.

Relatively new tools, such as markets and patient choice, are coming
to the fore. The key question is not which of these tools will deliver the
desired result, but rather what blend of them all is the right one in the
short to medium term (Dixon *et al* 2003). How the blend will be arrived
at will be a messy, haphazard, and not always rational process, based
in part on the factors noted above.

Further, it is quite possible that the NHS will benefit from a different
blend in different sectors. For example, it is arguable that developing a

market for the provision, or even commissioning, of elective surgery may be beneficial. After all, elective surgery is relatively discrete, generally uncomplicated and time limited, requiring only limited engagement of other services, and offering a choice of provider appears popular with patients. However, for chronic and emergency care, or highly specialist services such as cancer, the hallmark of good care can be collaboration between professionals in different institutions and across sectors. A market among providers may work less well in engineering this style of care. Instead, incentives that promote collaboration may be preferable.

In theory, although not in practice, primary care is the sector with the greatest tradition of competition for patients – patients can choose where they want to be treated but there is often not the capacity or willingness to allow this to happen. It is clear that more competition could be engineered within primary care: between practices as providers, and as commissioners. The imminent divestment by PCTs of their provision function, and their reorientation towards the commissioning of primary care (and, through primary care, other services) could encourage new suppliers of primary care, and may help to address the longstanding lack of capacity in this sector.

However, the introduction of competition in primary care is not without its complexities. For example, abandoning patient registration, as part of a strategy to increase competition within primary care, could undermine the continuity of doctor–patient relationships that may well deliver cost and quality benefits (Saultz and Lochner 2005). Similarly, the introduction of financial incentives to primary care professionals may clash with the intrinsic incentives to act professionally in the best interest of patients (Marshall and Harrison 2005).

As the NHS reforms are implemented, a number of possible scenarios can be foreseen:

Scenario 1: Market-based health care in provision and commissioning

Autonomous providers (arms-length NHS foundation institutions as well as those from the independent sector) would vie for contracts from commissioners, who themselves would compete for enrolled patients. Patients would choose their general practice, but also their 'health plan', which would act as the strategic accountable umbrella for practice-based commissioners. This market would be lightly regulated by one or more independent regulator, who would be responsible for ensuring that markets remained competitive, intervening only in the event of severe market instability that threatened the availability of essential services. Regulation would ensure that providers reached specified quality standards and would offer robust performance information upon which consumers could make choices.

Scenario 2: A tightly regulated market for NHS care provision

Here, competition between providers would be tempered by the requirement to participate in collaborative care networks (for example, for highly specialist services), overseen by PCTs in their evolving role as market managers. Further, explicit financial incentives would be introduced to foster collaboration between institutions. These would include additional fees under payment by results to reward cross-institutional objectives in managing chronic care. Independent regulators would take a more hands-on approach, assessing the performance of care across institutions. Regulation would go beyond that of financial management, and would include interventions to facilitate service improvement. Competition between commissioners would be limited, as now, to patient choice of general practice.

Scenario 3: A selective market for NHS care provision

In this scenario, dynamic market forces, in the shape of patient choice, a mixed economy of NHS and independent sector providers, and payment by results, would be applied differentially across services, such as to elective surgery and primary care. For other NHS services, a planning approach would be adopted, with practice-based commissioners, PCTs and providers acting in concert to design sustainable care pathways.

There are many variants of the simplified scenarios shown above. And the knock-ons could be even greater – for example, even affecting how aspects of health care are funded in the future. However, these thumb-nail sketches illustrate that a number of very different outcomes could result from the change agenda that has been initiated. They also raise an important question: can different approaches, with very different values underpinning each, co-exist within a single system? Can the NHS be 'diced and sliced' so that markets function happily in one sector, while collaborative planning is the norm in another?

Notwithstanding the attempts to separate out elective surgery from general NHS care (for example, through standalone surgical centres), the requirements of medical training, among other things, makes this difficult to achieve in practice – at least, at anything above a small scale. But if developing a coherent vision of an effective blend of levers is highly challenging, there is also the immediate and equally challenging agenda of effectively implementing the reforms already designed, and managing the risks that arise.

The scenarios detailed above also serve to expose different trade-offs between the fundamental aims of the NHS. The use of markets may increase producer efficiency and responsiveness to different patient needs, particularly in the elective care sector (although the formal evidence for this is limited). However, one cost of this efficiency could be a loss of equity as some consumers are able to make 'better' choices than others. Again, evidence to date on this important point is also limited (Coulter *et al* 2005, Burge *et al* 2005).

Moving forward

The government is forging ahead with its reform agenda for the NHS. With 2008 and the reduction in growth funding for the NHS looming, it will feel that it has little time to lose in implementing its planned changes. However, a significant number of failures and perceived cuts in NHS services may well present an obstacle to the reform process. It is clear that the emphasis on market incentives is uncomfortable for some within the Labour Party. In these circumstances, a return to 'command and control' may be the government's instinctive, or forced, reaction.

Yet it may be difficult to assess whether good progress is being made, given that the criteria for success are not entirely clear and there is bound to be a degree of turbulence in the implementation. One result of this may be that useful reforms are abandoned before they are able to prove their worth. The converse is also possible: that market reforms will continue but will prove inimical to the core aims of the NHS.

Government needs to make its medium-term vision for the NHS more transparent, and make sure that appropriate monitoring and evaluation mechanisms are in place to ensure that the reforms are moving the service in that direction.

At the King's Fund, we will be undertaking further analysis and research during the rest of 2005 and producing a series of publications and events to generate further debate and discussion about these important issues – in particular:

- the role of regulation in the new market
- how to strengthen commissioning and primary care
- getting the right mix of market incentives.

Details can be found on our website at:
www.kingsfund.org.uk/publications

References

Bamford T (2005). 'Anatomy of a meltdown'. *Health Service Journal*, vol 115, no 5967, pp 18–21.

Burge, P, Devlin N, Appleby J, Rohr C, Grant J (2005). *London Patient Choice Project Evaluation – A model of patients' choices of hospital from stated and revealed preference choice data*. Rand Europe: Cambridge.

Coulter A, Le Maistre N, Henderson L (2005). *Patients' Experience of Choosing Where to Undergo Surgical Treatment: Evaluation of London patient choice scheme*. London: Picker Institute.

Department of Health (2005a). 'Trend of actual growth expenditure on the NHS'. Table E2. Health and Personal Services Statistics website. Available at: www.performance.doh.gov.uk/HPSS (accessed on 26 August 2005)

Department of Health (2005b). *Commissioning a Patient-Led NHS*. London: Department of Health.

Department of Health (2000). *The NHS Plan: A plan for investment, a plan for reform*. London: The Stationery Office.

Department of Health (1998). *The Government's Expenditure Plans 1998–1999*. Departmental Report. London: Department of Health.

Dixon J, Le Grand J, Smith P (2003). *Can Market Forces be Used for Good?* London: King's Fund.

Healthcare Commission (2005). *NHS Performance Ratings 2004/5*. London: Healthcare Commission.

King's Fund (2005). *An Independent Audit of the NHS Under Labour (1997–2005)*. London: King's Fund.

Marshall M, Harrison S (2005). 'It's about more than money: financial incentives and internal motivation'. *Quality and Safety in Health Care*, vol 14, pp 4–5.
McFarland R (2005). 'Powerless to act'. *Health Service Journal*, vol 115, no 5967, pp 20–21.

Munro J, Nicholl J, O'Cathain A, Knowles E (2000). 'Impact of NHS Direct on demand for intermediate care: observational study'. *British Medical Journal*, vol 321, pp 150–53.

National Audit Office/Audit Commission (2005). *Financial Management in the NHS: NHS (England) summarised accounts 2003–04*. Report HC 600-1, session 2005–06. Norwich: The Stationery Office.

Saultz JW, Lochner J (2005). 'Interpersonal continuity of care and care outcomes: a critical review'. *Annals of Family Medicine*, vol 3, pp 159–66.

Wanless D (2002). *Securing Our Future Health: Taking a long-term view – The Wanless review*. Norwich: The Stationery Office.

Linked publications

We publish a wide range of resources on health and social care. See below for a selection. For our full range of titles, visit our website at **www.kingsfund.org.uk/publications** or call Sales and Information on 020 7307 2591.

Forthcoming titles

Regulation in the New NHS Market
Jennifer Dixon

The role of regulation in a market with a variety of health care providers – including NHS foundation hospitals, privately run diagnostic and treatment centres, and potentially staff-led primary care services – is likely to be quite different to that of the regulatory system we have today. Anticipating a further statutory review of health regulation, this paper will consider how best to combine economic and quality regulation, look at whether the new market can be managed to avoid major organisational failures, and review the roles of the various stakeholders.

October 2005 ISBN 1 85717 540 9 £5.00

Commissioning and Primary Care in the New NHS Market
Richard Lewis, Jennifer Dixon

Already the subject of a quiet revolution over the past few years – with the ending of the monopoly of provision by independently contracted GPs and the introduction of NHS Direct, walk-in centres and other new forms of first contact care – primary care is poised for further radical change. Central guidance on reforming the structure and roles of primary care trusts and enabling competition between primary care providers was issued this summer and a white paper on out-of-hospital care is expected at the turn of the year. This paper will look at how commissioning can be strengthened and whether competition has a useful role.

November 2005 ISBN 1 85717 536 0 £5.00

Incentives in the New NHS Market
Rebecca Rosen, Anthony Harrison, Jenny Grant

While incentives to maximise productivity and reduce waiting times may be appropriate for elective care, they are less useful – and may even be deleterious – for emergency care and services for patients with long-term conditions. Here, the avoidance of hospitalisation may be a more appropriate aim, yet commissioners, primary care providers and NHS trusts do not have strong incentives to work towards this aim. This paper will consider how best to design appropriate incentives for different parts of the health care system to ensure that perverse impacts are anticipated and minimised.

December 2005 ISBN 1 85717 537 9 £5.00

Published titles

An Independent Audit of the NHS Under Labour (1997–2005)
King's Fund

The Labour Party came to power in 1997 promising to 'save' the NHS. Since then it has invested unprecedented levels of funding in the health service, but has emphasised that the extra money must be linked to 'reform'. This audit, commissioned by *The Sunday Times*, assesses the Labour government's performance against its targets to bring down waiting times; recruit more health care professionals; and improve care in cancer, heart disease and mental health.

March 2005 ISBN 1 85717 488 7 88 pages £20.00

Practice-Led Commissioning: Harnessing the power of the primary care frontline
Richard Lewis

Practice-led commissioning – which involves primary care clinicians in commissioning care and services – could help meet two challenges. First, it could boost the strength of commissioning. Second, it could harness the talents of clinicians in managing and planning health services. This paper looks at the benefits of practice-led commissioning, and what it could mean within the new NHS structures. It explores the lessons of GP fundholding, total purchasing, and locality/GP commissioning pilots. Finally, it looks at ways of implementing practice-led commissioning, highlighting strategic risks and identifying where practice-led commissioning would be most welcome.

June 2004 ISBN 1 85717 506 9 32 pages £5.00

Government and the NHS: Time for a new relationship?
Steve Dewar

A range of public services, including higher education, housing, and public service broadcasting, are now being funded, delivered, or regulated through agencies working at arm's length from government. This paper looks at the conceptual and practical challenges – as well as the potential benefits – of arm's-length governance for the NHS, reviews past arguments, and considers how a new arm's-length NHS agency, accountable to Parliament, could work with government to improve health care. It argues that such an agency could make the NHS more accountable, transparent, and inclusive while also freeing up the government to consider the impact of factors, such as housing and education, on health.

October 2003 ISBN 1 85717 481 x 62 pages £6.50

What Is the Real Cost of More Patient Choice?
John Appleby, Anthony Harrison, Nancy Devlin

At first glance, an increase in patient choice seems to be unequivocally 'a good thing'. But what trade-offs are really involved – and what price are we prepared to pay? And how far can individual freedoms be extended while retaining the essential objectives of the NHS? This discussion paper sets out the questions that the government needs to answer if it wants to place patient choice at the heart of a health care system funded by tax-payers. These include how extra costs will be met, whether patients are willing and able to exercise choice in their own best interests, and what kinds of limits to choice might be needed.

June 2003 ISBN 1 85717 473 9 64 pages £6.50

Can Market Forces be Used for Good?
Jennifer Dixon, Julian Le Grand, Peter Smith

The government is committed to changing the NHS and making services more responsive to public demands. Meanwhile, there is ongoing debate about the benefits of market disciplines versus planned provision. This paper asks whether a highly centralised system can sit comfortably alongside a market-led approach, and whether market forces can respond effectively to demands of an ageing population. It brings together the views of three expert commentators: Julian Le Grand says stronger market incentives would improve performance among secondary care providers; Peter Smith argues against even modest experimentation with stronger market incentives; and Jennifer Dixon looks at the possibility of combining the best aspects of market disciplines with planned provision.

May 2003 ISBN 1 85717 477 1 49 pages £6.50

Future Directions for Primary Care Trusts
Richard Lewis, Jennifer Dixon, Stephen Gillam

The government has set out demanding modernisation plans for the NHS. It wants providers to be more responsive to patients, and market excesses to be curbed by better regulation and new models of social ownership. Meanwhile primary care trusts (PCTs) have been struggling to rise to the challenge. As a result, two new policy themes have emerged: stronger market incentives and decentralisation of budgetary power. This paper looks at how PCTs can adapt to these new policies and strengthen their commissioning role.

May 2003 ISBN 1 85717 513 1 16 pages £5.00